My Awesome PAPA

I Wrote a book about you

THIS BOOK IS WRITTEN BY

_____

Here is my Grandpa!

Three words I would use to describe him are

_____,

_____ and

_____!

If my grandad was a superhero, his power would be

_____

_____

I admire my grandpa because

_____

_____

_____

_____

When I think of my Grandpa, I think of

_____

_____

_____

_____

My grandapa knows how to _____ _____ better than anyone.

When I need help with
_____,
I ask my grandpa.

My grandpa always tells the story of the time when

_____

_____

_____

_____

I'm thankful for my grandpa because

_____

_____

_____

My grandpa makes
me laugh when

_____

_____

_____

_____

My grandpa and I
_____
_____ when
we spend time
together.

I show my grandpa appreciation by

_____

_____

_____

When I get older, I hope my grandpa and I can _____

_____

_____

_____

People that know my grandpa say he

_____

_____

_____

Something not many people know about my grandpa is

_____,

The most important lesson my grandpa ever taught me

_____

_____

_____

On Father's Day, I want my grandpa to know

_____

_____

____

Elkreativ
PUBLISHING

Made in United States
Cleveland, OH
02 June 2025